THIS WALKER BOOK BELONGS TO:

_____

_____

_____

_____

For Andrés

First published 1999 by Walker Books Ltd
87 Vauxhall Walk, London SE11 5HJ

This edition published 2003

4 6 8 10 9 7 5 3

Text © 1999 Walker Books Ltd
Illustrations © 1999 Ana Martín Larrañaga

This book has been typeset in ITC Highlander

Printed in Hong Kong

British Library Cataloguing in Publication Data:
a catalogue record for this book is
available from the British Library

ISBN 0-7445-9484-7

The Big Wide-Mouthed Frog

A Traditional Tale

Illustrated by

Ana Martín Larrañaga

WALKER BOOKS
AND SUBSIDIARIES
LONDON · BOSTON · SYDNEY

Once there was a big
wide-mouthed frog with
the biggest, widest mouth
you ever did see.

And one day that big wide-mouthed frog hopped off to see the world.

The first creature he met
had big thumping feet.

"Hey, you! Big Thumping Feet!
  Who are you and what do you eat?"
  shouted the wide-mouthed frog.
"I'm a kangaroo," said Kangaroo,
"and I eat grass."
"Well, I'm a big wide-mouthed frog!"
  shouted the wide-mouthed frog.
"And I eat flies!"

The second creature
he met had a big
black nose.

"Listen, Mister Big Nose!
Who are you and what do you eat?"
shouted the wide-mouthed frog.

"I'm a koala," said Koala,
"and I eat leaves."
"Well, I'm a big wide-mouthed frog!"
shouted the wide-mouthed frog.
"And I eat flies!"

The third
creature
he met was
hanging
upside down.

"Ho there,
   Upside-down Creature!
   Who are you and what do you eat?"
   shouted the wide-mouthed frog.
"I'm a possum," said Possum,
"and I eat blossom."
"Well, I'm a big wide-mouthed frog!"
   shouted the wide-mouthed frog.
"And I eat flies!"

The fourth creature he met
had three long toes.
"Look here, Three Long Toes!
Who are you and what do you eat?"
shouted the wide-mouthed frog.

"I'm an emu," said Emu,
"and I eat grasshoppers."
"Well, I'm a big wide-mouthed frog!"
shouted the wide-mouthed frog.
"And I eat flies!"

Then the wide-mouthed frog met a creature stretched out on the riverbank like a knobbly brown log.

"HEY, Knobbly Brown Log! Who are you and what do you eat?" shouted the wide-mouthed frog.

Knobbly Brown Log opened
her mouth in a slow, wide,
lazy smile.

"Good day to you, too," she said. "I'm a crocodile and I eat big wide-mouthed frogs. Who are you and what do you eat?"

"Me?" whispered the wide-mouthed frog, puckering his mouth into the smallest, narrowest mouth you ever did see.

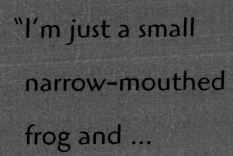

"I'm just a small narrow-mouthed frog and ..."

I'm